Collins

Cherry Blossoms

Art and Craft

LKG

FS2

SERIES EDITOR: RANI THIPPAVAZZULA

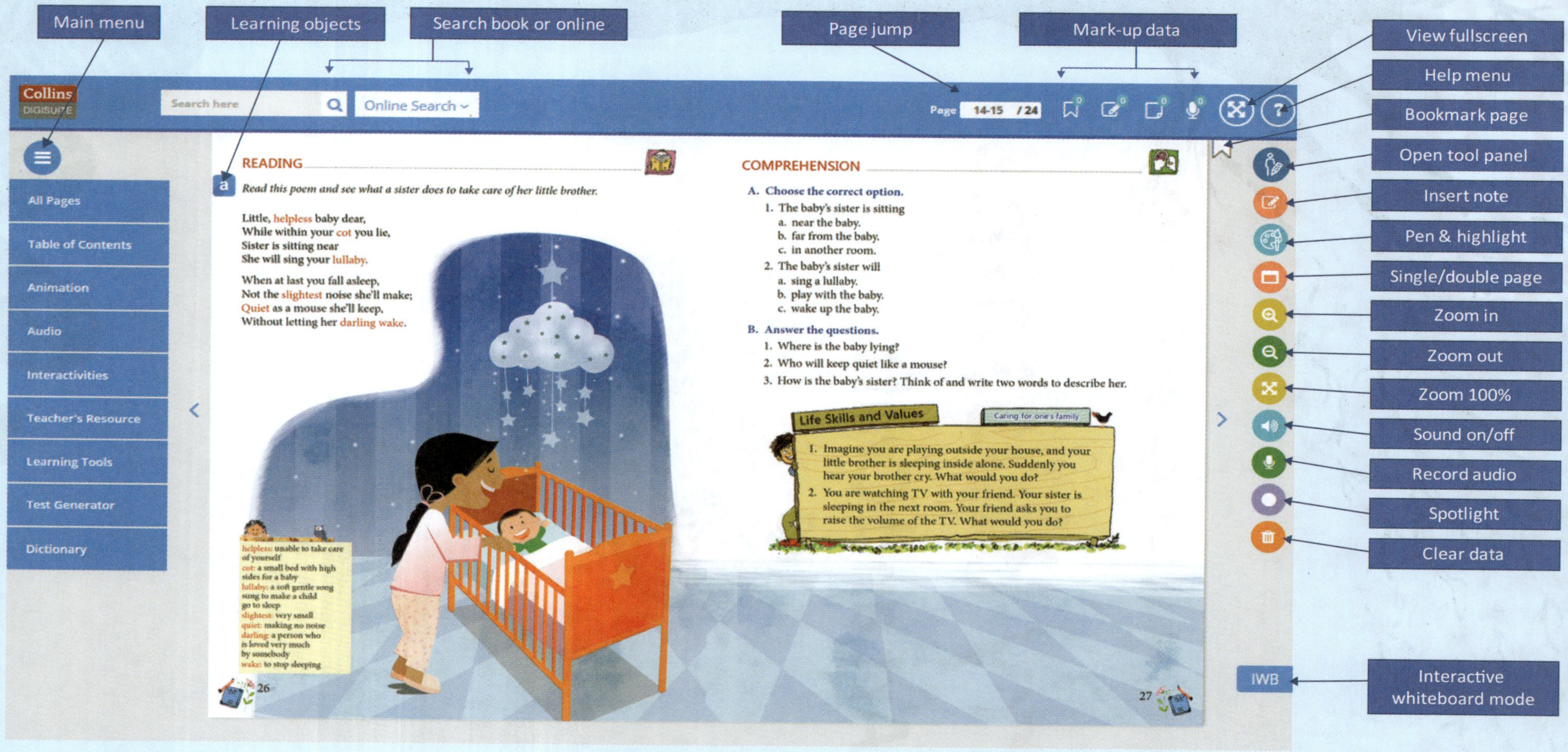

Student + Teacher						Teacher-only			
a	animations	ia	activities	g	games	lp	lesson plans	tn	teacher's notes
ilt	instructor-led tutorials	w	worksheets	v	videos	w	worksheets	ak	answer keys
		(audio icon)	audio						

Preface

Cherry Blossoms provides graded, age-appropriate learning opportunities targeting holistic skill development for children in the age group of 3 years to 8 years. The series aligns with the vision outlined in the National Education Policy, 2020 for early years. It spreads across five levels, Nursery (Foundational Stage 1) to Class 2 (Foundational Stage 5). The books use a combination of hands-on activities, frequent recapitulation and child-friendly artwork to facilitate learning.

The series comprises **40 books** and spans **English**, **Maths**, **General Awareness**, and **Art and Craft**. The series comes bundled with a **workbook** for each subject and a book of **rhymes** and **stories** for Foundational Stage 1 to 3.

This series integrates the essence of **NIPUN Bharat** guidelines, which extensively deal with Foundational Literacy and Numeracy. The series aims to motivate learners to read independently, to improve their vocabulary, number sense and spatial understanding. The **Foundational Literacy and Numeracy (FLN)** skills include the skills for developing their critical thinking, logical reasoning and creative skills, as well as the skills to enhance their ability to express themselves both verbally and in writing.

Cherry Blossoms Teacher Support Materials include:

Teacher's Resource Books: Comprises stories, activity banks, classroom management and assessment guidelines

Multimedia eBook: Consists of animations, audio, video, slide shows, and interactive exercises

Print-ready Worksheets: Additional worksheets for practice and reinforcement, present in the digital support

Digital Flashcards: Flashcards with embedded sounds and animations for letter formation and letter-sound association

Animations and Songs: Animated stories and rhymes set to tune

Interactive Games: Interactivities to reinforce concepts in a fun and engaging manner

A note on the activity banks (included in the Teacher's Manuals)

The activity banks comprise hands-on activities that will help children develop the requisite skills to attain age-appropriate learning goals. In keeping with Howard Gardener's theory of multiple intelligences, the activity banks include options and variations that enable teachers to provide a planned cycle of experiences and opportunities, which foster each type of intelligence, to every child in their classrooms. The activity banks equip teachers to use the strengths of children as a means of complementing their less developed areas by valuing and nurturing the inherent abilities of the children.

Rani Thippavazzula, former Academic Director, Ravindra Bharathi Group is an eminent educationist with over two decades of experience in teaching, administration and curriculum design and development. As an Academic Advisor for chain schools pan India, she is proficient in developing learning products and is a specialist in Differentiated Instruction, Enterprise Education and Early Childhood Education.

Learning and Development During the Early Years

The early years are the most significant years for growth, development and learning. During this period, children need adequate opportunities for stimulating experiences as these favourably affect various learning abilities. Learning experiences, when chosen and planned properly, fuel the innate curiosity of children, and stimulate their thought processes.

The goal of learning during the early years is to enhance the all-round development of personality and to inculcate healthy attitudes, life skills and good values. Creative play, well thought-out games and developmentally appropriate activities help children develop the necessary skills to achieve these goals. The skills that children need to acquire can broadly be categorized as:

Motor:
Motor skills pertain not only to gross motor activities like walking and jumping but also include fine motor activities like the ability to hold a pencil and write. The development of motor skills is facilitated through several graded activities.

Personal, Social and Emotional:
Personal, social and emotional development, necessary for the overall personality development of children, is achieved using a combination of hands-on activities, role plays and thought-provoking stories and rhymes.

Linguistic:
The ability to listen, speak, read and write is critical to success in formal learning environments.

Mathematical:
The development of mathematical ideas and concepts is important at this stage since children will continue to build on this learning for most of their years of schooling.

Knowledge and Understanding of the World:
This is achieved through activities that enable children to explore their surroundings at home and in the school, and interact with the people that they see around them.

Health and Safety: The idea of health and safety is introduced through activities, stories and retelling of real-life experiences to encourage children to focus on health and well-being.

Creative:
Creative skills are developed through a host of activities involving art, craft, painting, roleplays, etc.

Logical and Rational Thinking:
Activities that involve simple puzzles, pattern-completion and visual discrimination help children to develop logical and rational thinking skills.

Contents

WALKTHROUGH

A variety of tracing and colouring activities to further fine motor development in an enjoyable manner

Free-hand drawing and colouring pages to support creative development

Rolling, flattening and shaping modelling clay and cotton to support motor development

Tearing, pasting, cutting to improve hand-eye coordination and develop the ability to grip objects

Cross-curricular linkages in activities to help support overall learning development

LUMINOUS LAMP

Make a lamp with the letter L. Decorate it as you like.

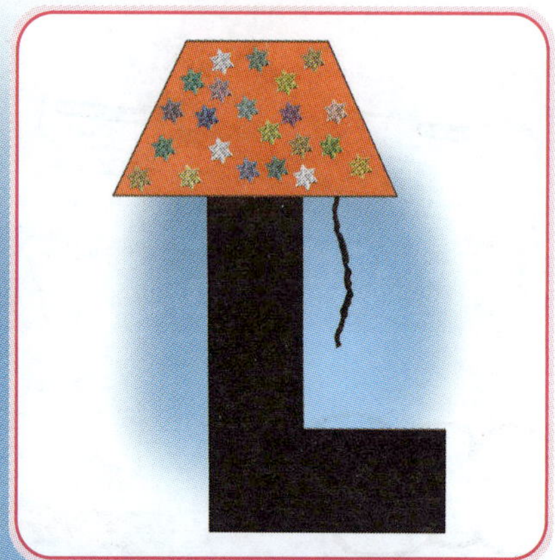

Material Required

Orange/yellow origami paper, child-safe scissors, black wool, decorative material and glue

Procedure

Draw the shape of the lampshade on the origami paper. Encourage children to cut the paper along the lines independently. Children should paste black wool next to the letter 'L'. Paste the paper in the space provided. Allow children to decorate the lampshade as they like.

CUTE CATERPILLAR

Paste woollen threads in spirals to make the caterpillar.

Procedure

Help children cut wool into small pieces. Encourage children to paste the wool independently. Demonstrate how to paste the lengths of wool in a spiral manner.

Material Required

Woollen threads, child-safe scissors, and glue

UNDERWATER WORLD

Use pencil colours to colour the animals. Count and write the number of animals.

Procedure

Allow children to colour all the animals. They can use any colour they like. Make sure that they use a single colour for one kind of creature. They can then count and use pencil colours to write number of each creatures in the aquarium.

Material Required

Pencil colours

CLUCK-CLUCK CHICKS

Print your hands to make chicks.

Procedure

Demonstrate how to dip the hand in yellow paint and print on the paper. Children should be guided to place their thumbs just below the crowns of hens.

Material Required

Yellow poster colour and black sketch pen

SHAPE ROCKET

Make a rocket with different shapes.

Procedure

Encourage children to cut out the required shapes of origami paper to make a rocket. To show the trail of smoke coming out of the rocket, children can paste cotton at the bottom edge of the rocket. To make clouds, they can be asked to paste cotton again. They can decorate the rocket with decorative material as they like.

Material Required

Origami paper, cotton, decorative material, child-safe scissors and glue

MY FRUIT BASKET

Complete the fruit basket. Colour the details of fruits.

Procedure

Explain that a different method is used to make each fruit. Cut and paste red origami paper to make the apple. Paste lengths of yellow wool to make the banana. Thumbprint using purple/ green poster colour to make the grapes. Use crayons to colour the pineapple. Use maroon sparkle to make the cherries.

Material Required

Yellow wool, red origami paper, crayons, purple/ green poster colour, maroon sparkle, child-safe scissors and glue

COLOURFUL CANOPY

Use cotton to rainbow paint the umbrella.

Procedure

Demonstrate how to dip cotton in different poster colours and make a colourful umbrella.

Material Required

Poster colours, cotton

THE QUEEN'S DRESS

Use okra to print the dress of the queen.

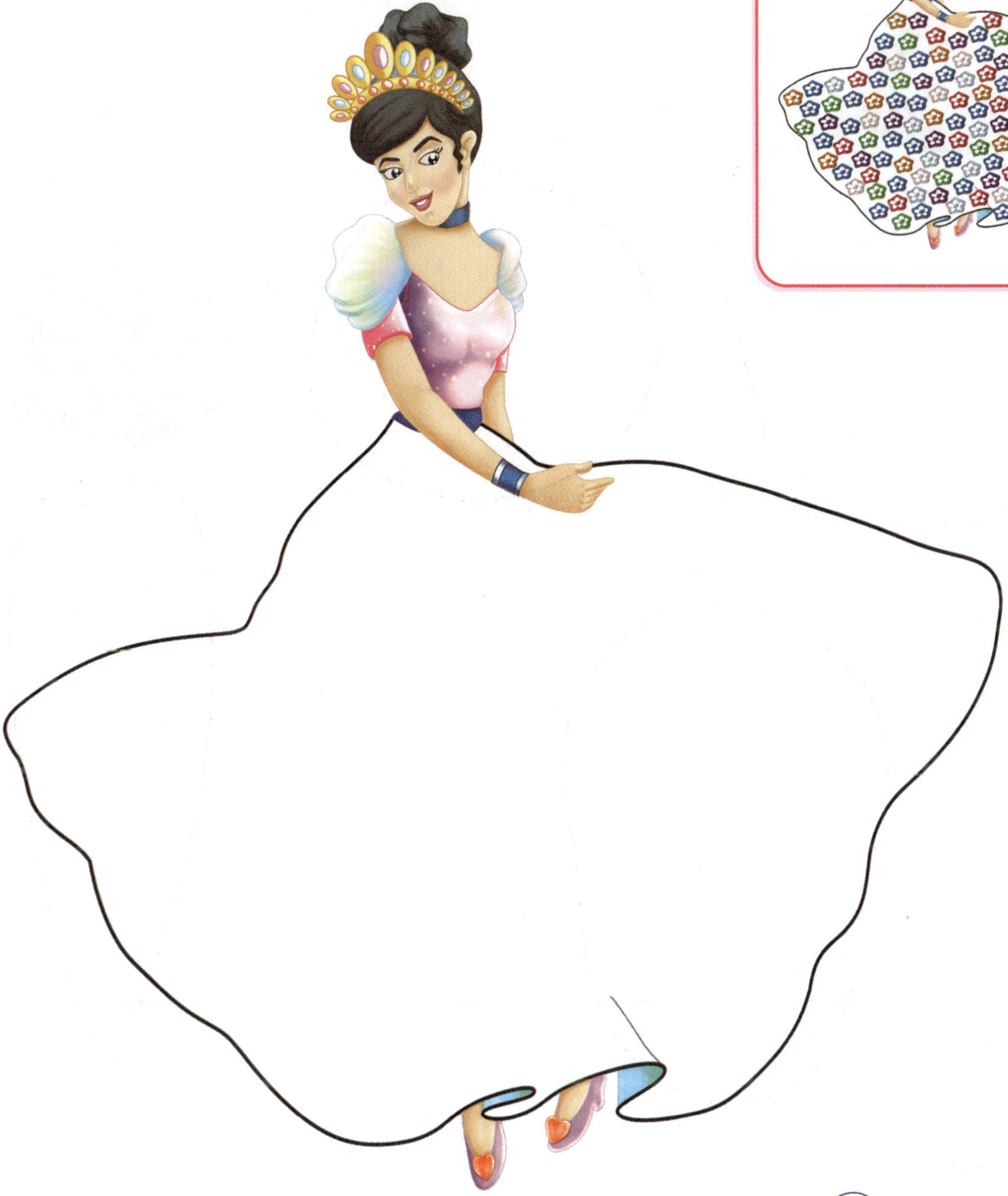

Procedure

Demonstrate how to dip the cut okra in paint and print to make the dress of the queen.

Material Required

2-3 pieces of okra and poster colours

VEGGIES

Create a veggie family using pencil colours.

Procedure

Children should use relevant pencil colour to draw curves and loops for each vegetable. Encourage children to do the activity independently. After they finish doing the activity, ask them to name each vegetable.

Material Required

Pencil colours

ORIGAMI KITE

Make a kite using origami paper.

Step 1

Step 2

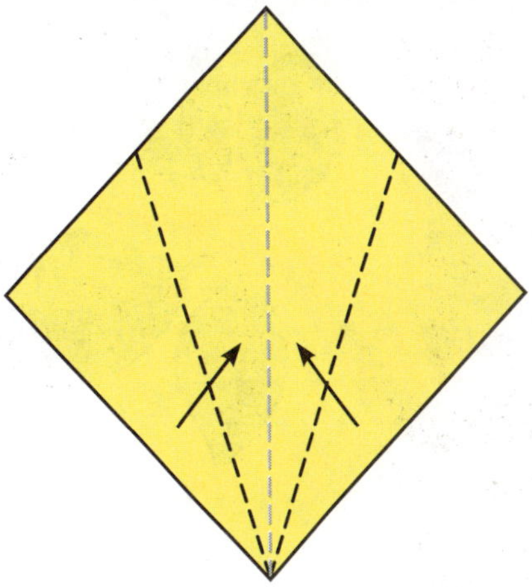

Step 3

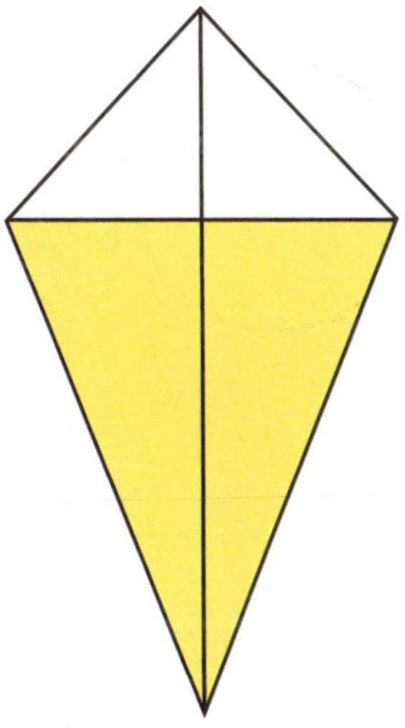

Paste here

Procedure

Follow steps to make a kite. Paste the kite and decorate it with differently coloured sketch pens.

Material Required

Origami paper, sketch pens and glue

GIRAFFE

Use a dice to make spots on the giraffe. Paste brown wool to make giraffe's tail.

Material Required

A dice, brown poster colours, brown/orange wool and glue

Procedure

Children can be asked to bring a dice. They can dip the dice in brown poster colour and print the impression on the hollow marks to make spots on the giraffe. They should paste wool preferably of orange/brown colour for the tail of the giraffe.

LET'S DRAW!

Draw and colour anything you like.

JUMBO ELEPHANT

B – Y –
G – R –

Let's make an elephant.

Procedure

Colour the elephant as per the given colour code.

Material Required

Crayons

SPRAY PAINTING

Spray paint to complete the tree.

Material Required

Poster colours—green, red and brown, a toothbrush and water

Procedure

Demonstrate how to spray paint the tree using a toothbrush. To paint apples, children can smudge red paint with their index fingers and water. While doing this activity, they can cover the page with a newspaper or any rough cloth to minimize the spread of colours at unwanted places.

SPOTTY FLOWER

Make the flower. Decorate the flower as you like.

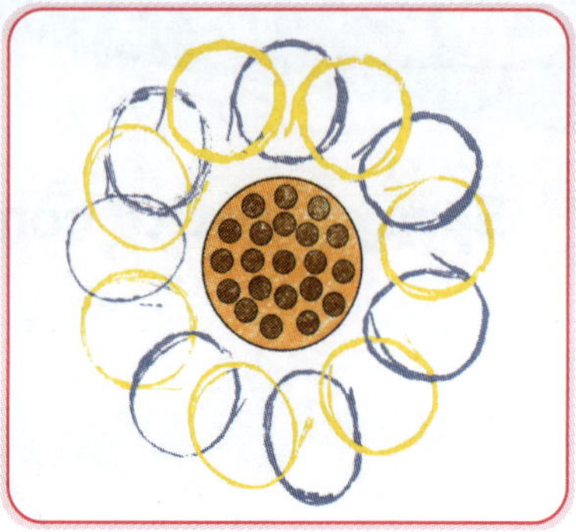

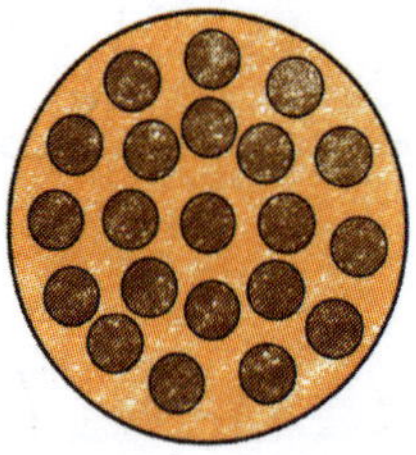

Procedure

Help children roll any A4 sheet and staple its edges. Use a paper plate to pour any poster colour in it for easy dipping and printing of the paper roll to make an impression of the flower. They can use both sides of the paper roll to make two-coloured flower by printing each side with different colour.

Material Required

1 A4 paper, any poster colour, stapler and a paper plate

ICY OCTOPUS

Let's make an octopus with paper folding.

Procedure

Demonstrate how to make a big hollow capital letter 'O' on a chart paper. Children can cut and paste the letter on the page. They should cut lengths of (blue) A4 sheet to fold the paper back and forth multiple times and make tentacles of the octopus. In the end, they can use black sketch pen to make eyes of the octopus.

Material Required

Blue chart paper, 1 A4 blue paper, child-safe scissors and glue

STRAW HUT

Use ice-cream sticks and paper straw to make a hut.

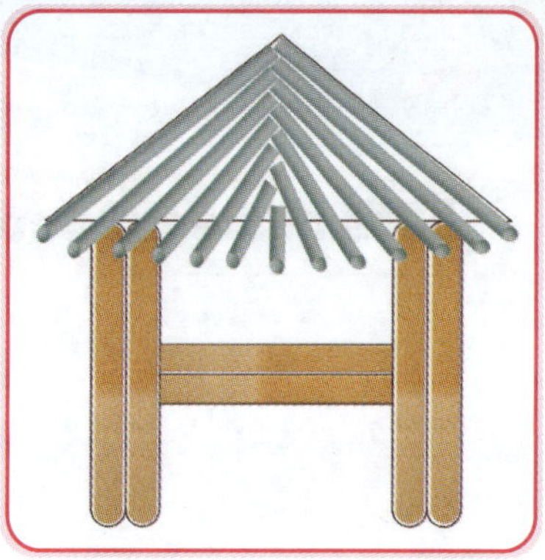

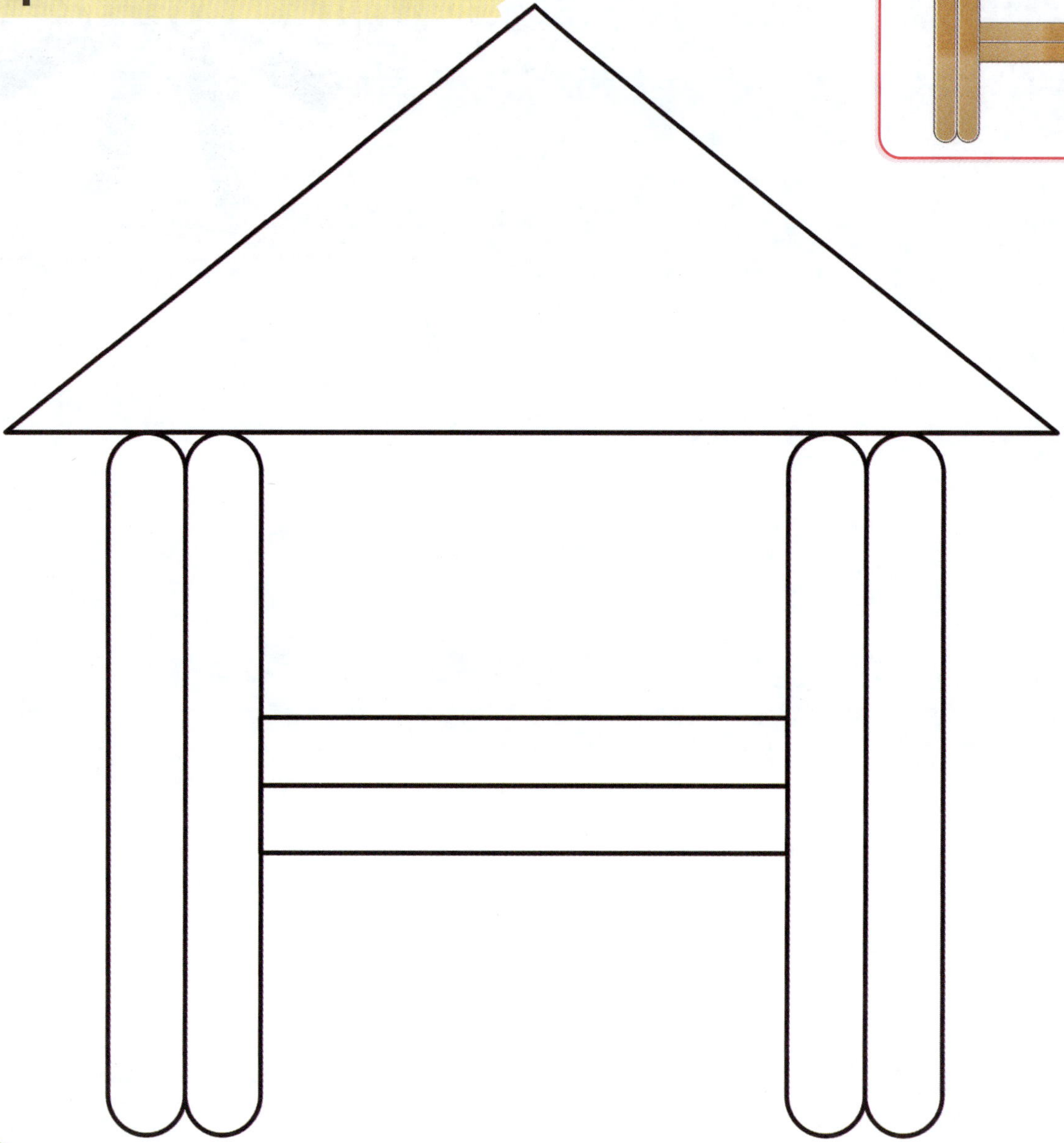

Procedure

Paint ice-cream sticks brown and paste those sticks on the hollow letter 'H' just as shown in the sample image. Paste paper straws over the top of the letter 'H' to complete the hut. Children can colour the ice-cream sticks using brown poster colour.

Material Required

Ice-cream sticks, paper straws, paintbrush, child-safe scissors, glue and brown poster colour

SAND ART

Complete the scenery with sand. Use crayons to colour the other objects.

Material Required

Crayons, sand and glue

Procedure

First, colour the tree and the hut. Then, apply glue on the path to the hut to put sand on it.

ORIGAMI CAT

Make the face of a cat using origami paper.

Step 1

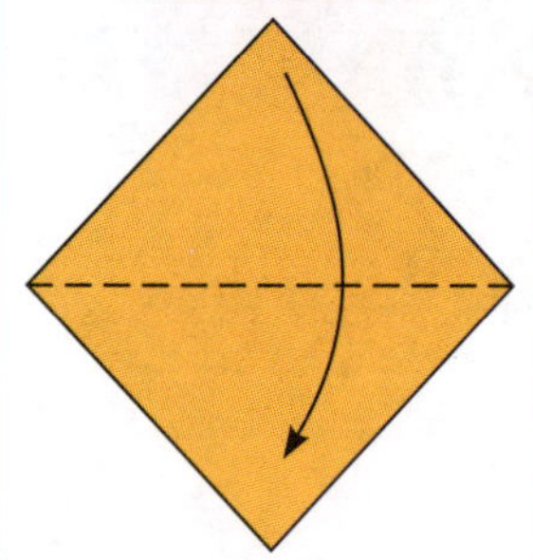

Step 2

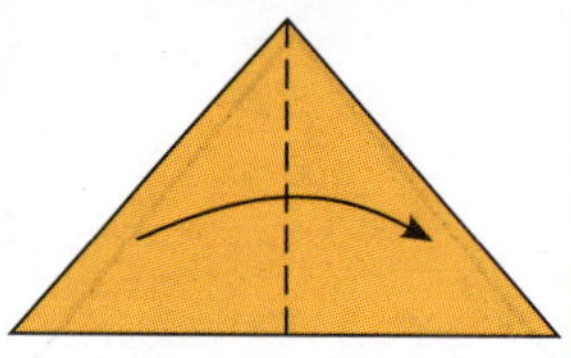

Step 3

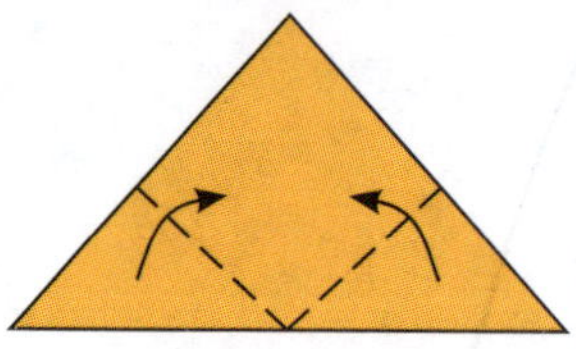

Step 4

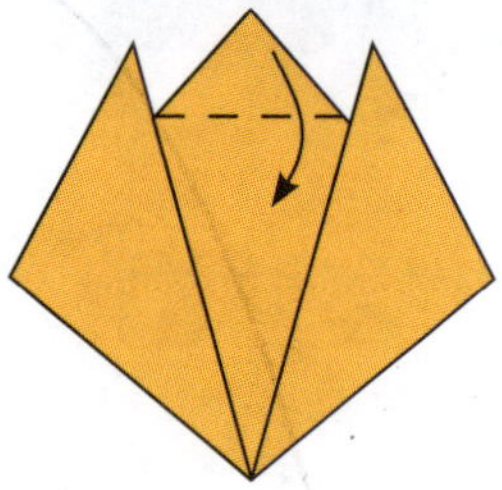

Step 5

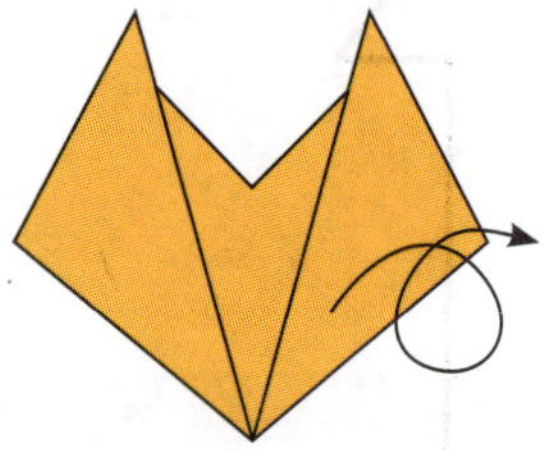

Step 6

Paste here

Procedure

Follow the steps to make the cat using origami paper. Use a black sketch pen to make the nose and the whiskers. Paste googly eyes to complete the cat.

Material Required

Origami paper, black sketch pen, googly eyes and glue

PROUD PEACOCK

Colour and decorate the peacock.

Procedure

Using blue and green crayons, colour the head, legs, feet, and some portion of the tail of the peacock. Paste colourful beads/stickers in the same sequence/pattern as shown in the reference image.

Material Required

Colourful beads/ decorative stickers, glue, blue and green crayons

WRIGGLY WORM

Make a worm with the letter 'W'.

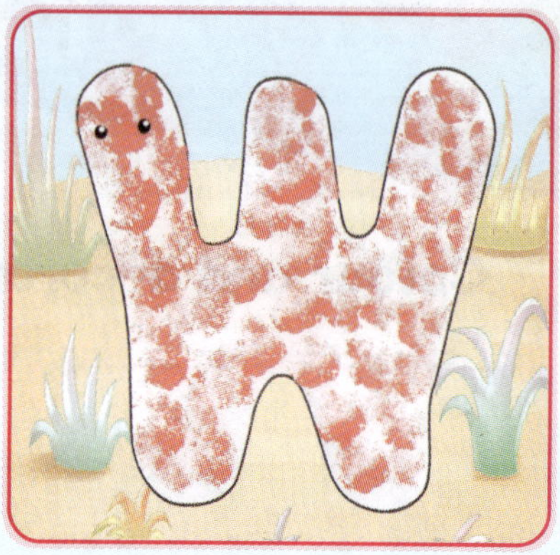

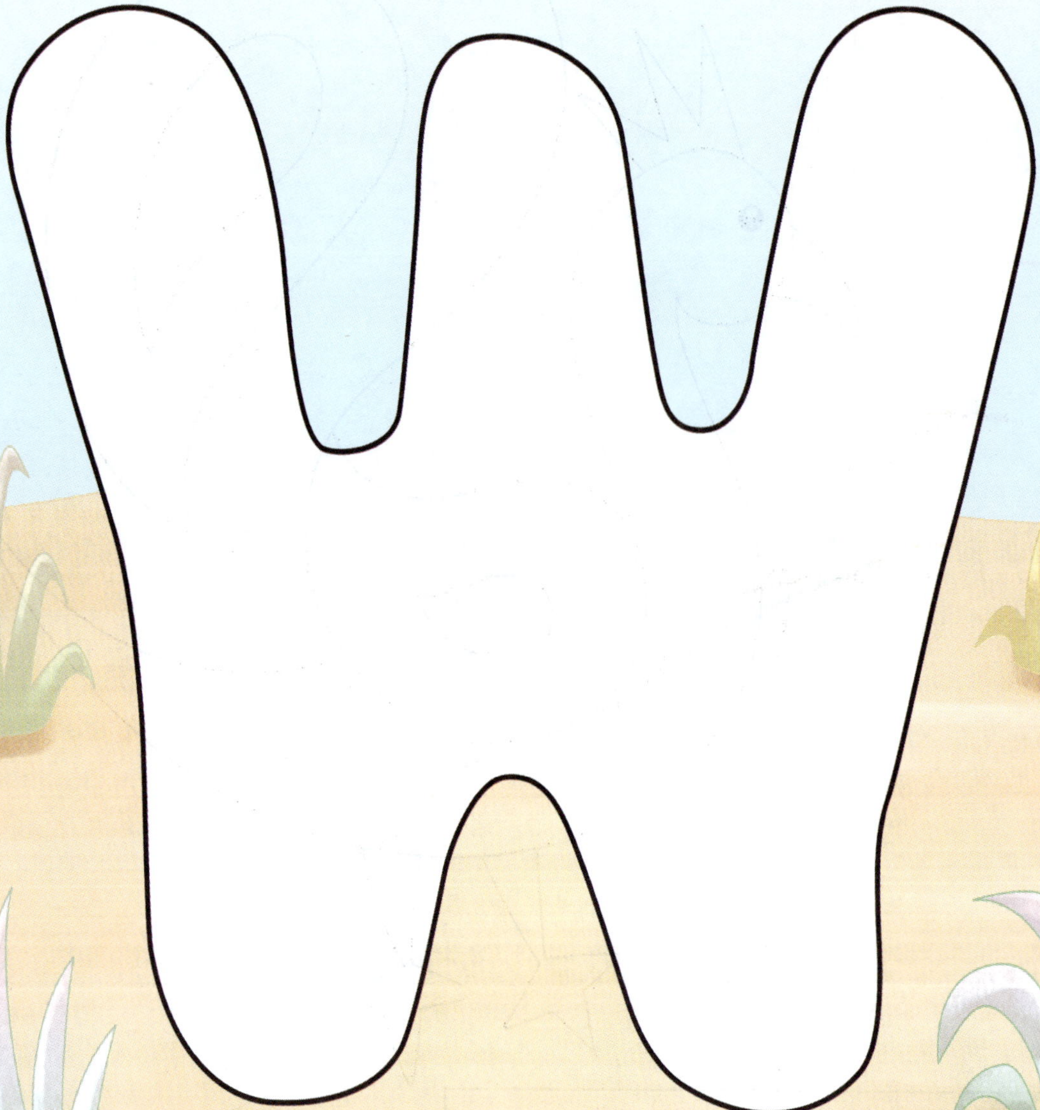

Procedure

Demonstrate how children can use a wooden peg to hold cotton and do the dip and print activity. They should then use black sketch pen to make the eye of the worm.

Material Required

1 wooden cloth peg, cotton and poster colours

LET'S DRAW!

Draw and colour anything you like.

CHIRPING BIRDS

Thumbprint to make birds on the tree.

Procedure

Thumbprint with different poster colours to make birds on the branches of the tree. Use a black sketch pen to make their eyes, beaks, claws and tail as shown in the reference image.

Material Required

2-3 poster colours, and black sketch pen

DRAW WITH NUMBERS

Draw and colour the shark.

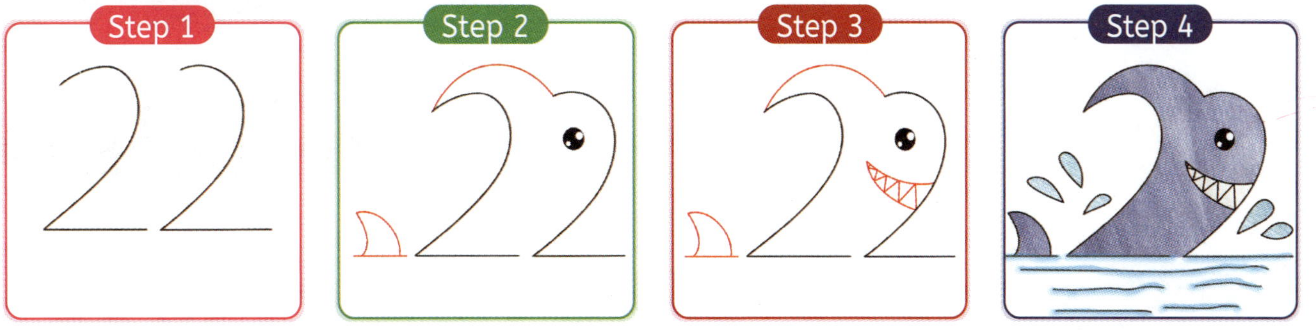

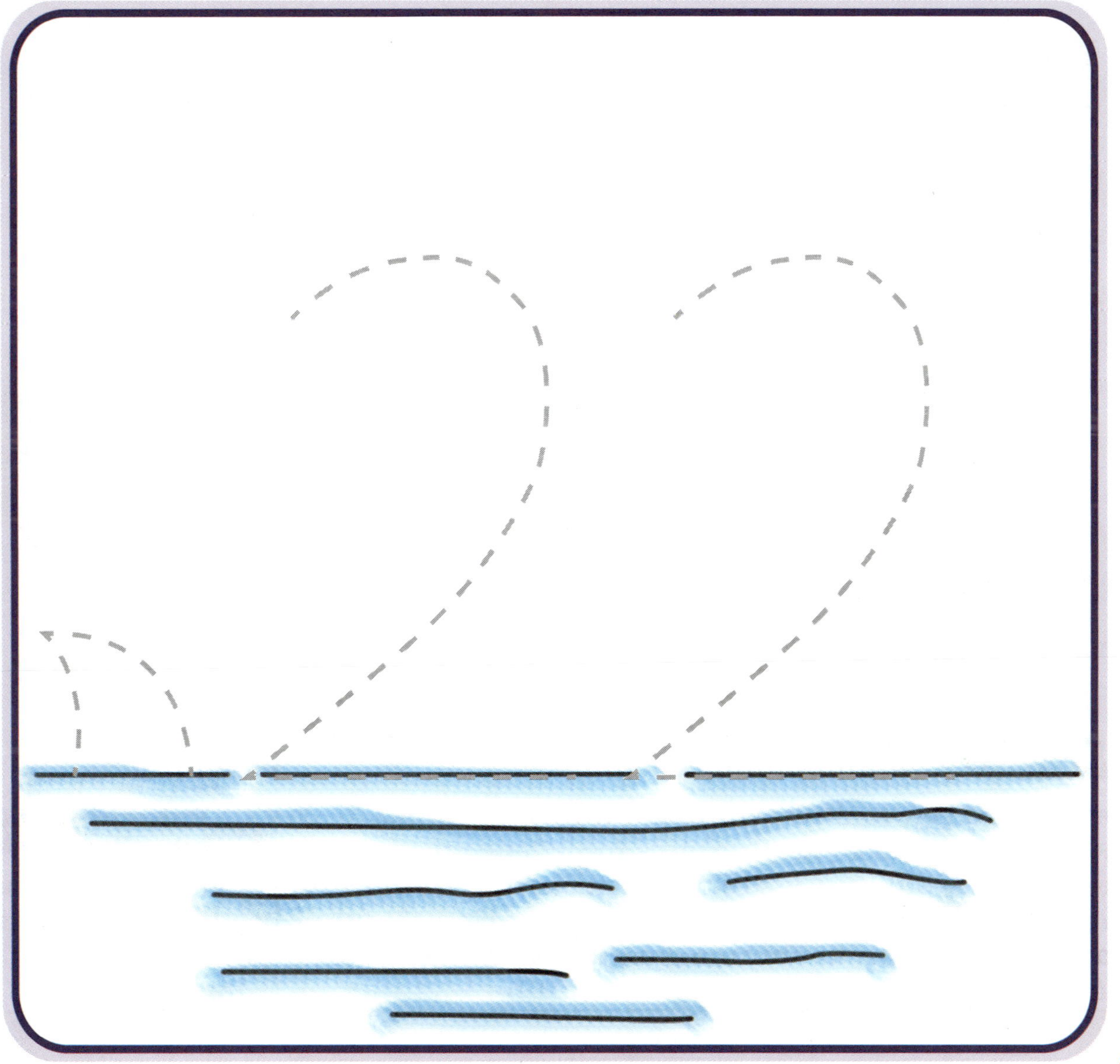

UNDERWATER CREATURES

Use felt paper to make underwater creatures.

Procedure

Demonstrate how to draw and cut out the hollow capital 'U' on the felt paper. Children can then place the letter on the centre of the page. They can again use coloured felt paper to cut shapes of circles, ovals and triangles to make fish. They can place the fish on and around the letter 'U'. They can draw the eyes of the fish using a black sketch pen.

Material Required

Sheets of felt paper, child-safe scissors, black sketch pen and glue

ORIGAMI COW

Make the face of a cow using origami paper.

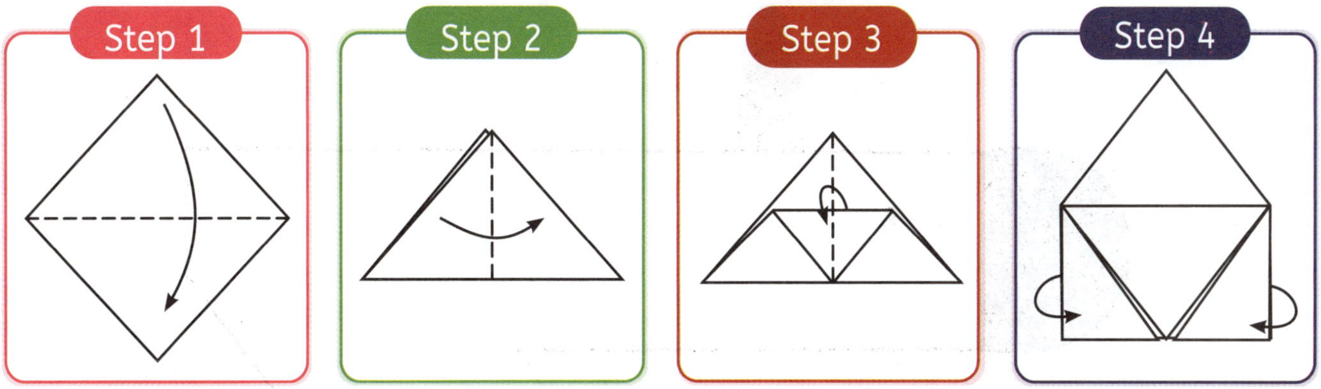

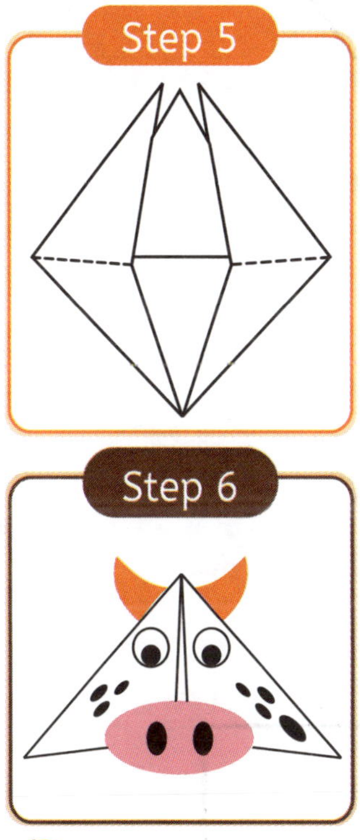

Paste here

Procedure

Follow the steps to make the cow using white paper. Children can then cut pink origami paper to make the nose of the cow. To make horns of the cow, they can cut and paste orange origami paper on the cow (refer to the image given above). Use black sketch pen to make eyes and black spots on the cow. Once they are done with making the origami cow, they can paste it on the page.

Material Required

A4-size white paper, pink and orange origami paper, black sketch pen, child-safe scissors, and glue

STRIPY ZEBRA

Paste strips of black paper and lengths of black wool to make the zebra.

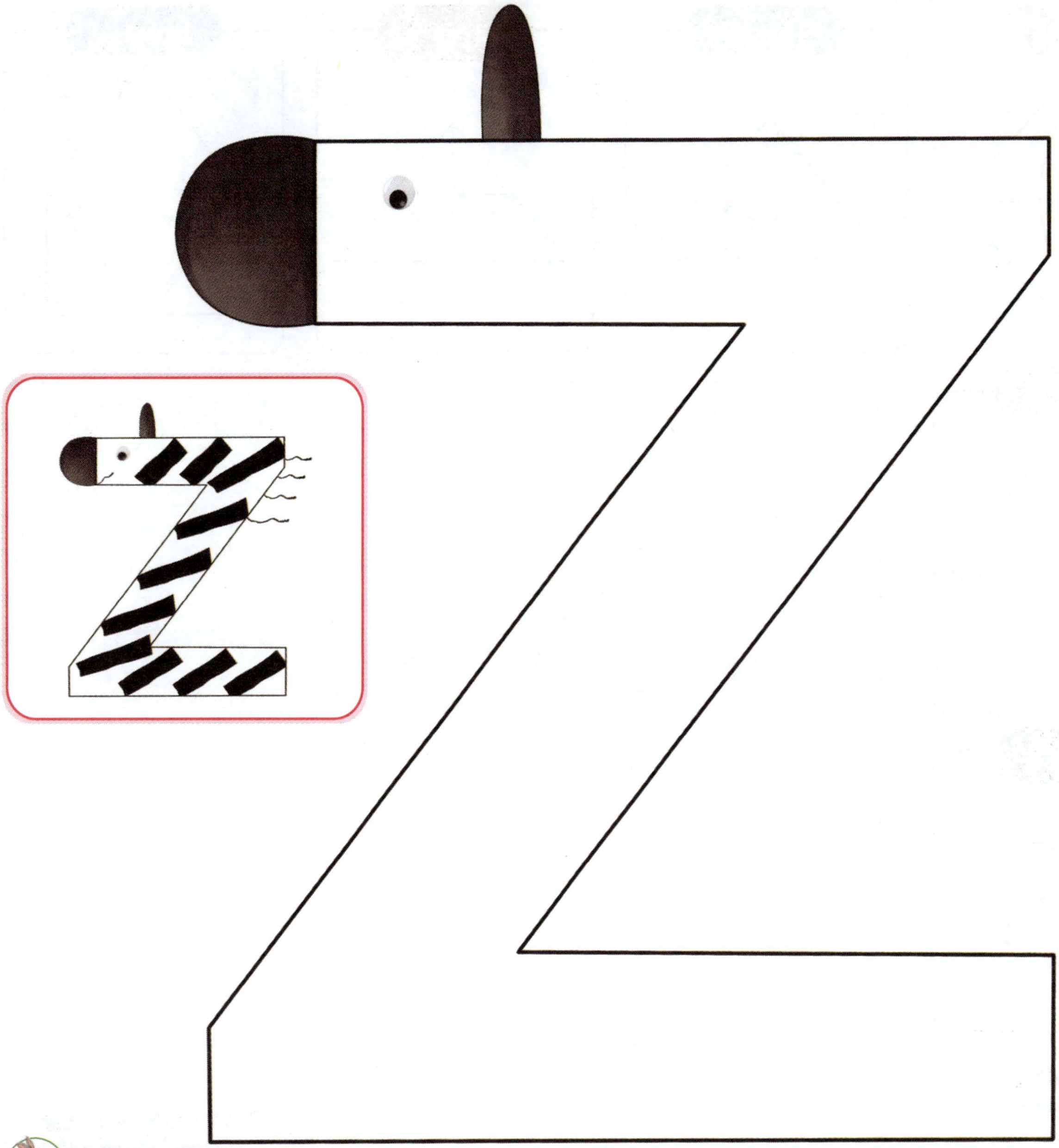

Procedure

Demonstrate how to cut thick but short strips of black paper and paste it on the letter. Children can then paste pieces of black wool on the zebra to make its hair. They can also use a small piece of wool to make a smile on the zebra's face.

Material Required

Black paper, child-safe scissors, black wool, black sketch pen and glue

PALM PARROT

Make colourful feathers of the parrot.

Material Required

Sheets of coloured A4 paper, child-safe scissors and glue

Procedure

Ask children to trace their hands on three differently coloured sheets. Cut out the hand print. Demonstrate how to paste them. For the first cut-out, fold it into equal halves and paste it little towards the end of the parrot's tail so that it is visible and is not overlapped by other sheets that are yet to be pasted for feathers. For the second and third cut-outs, cut those in two equal halves and paste the coloured sheets alternately to complete the colourful feathers of the parrot. Use the thumbnail to guide the pasting of the feather.

ORIGAMI DOG

Make the face of a dog using origami paper.

Step 1

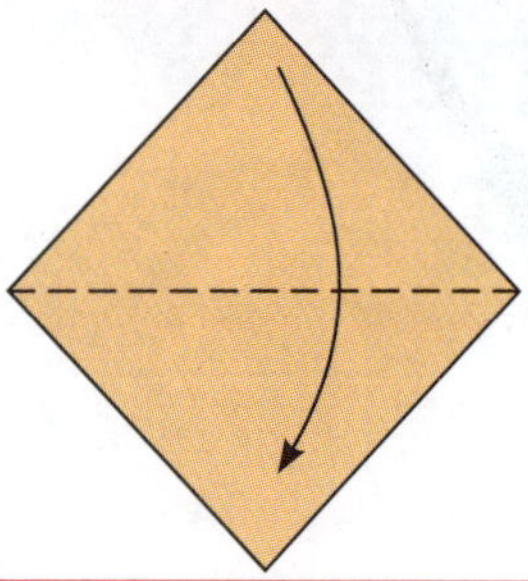

Step 2

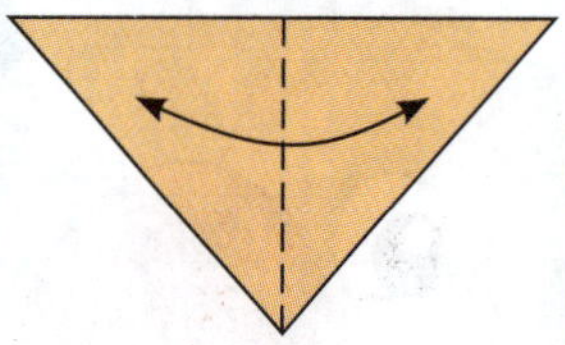

Step 3

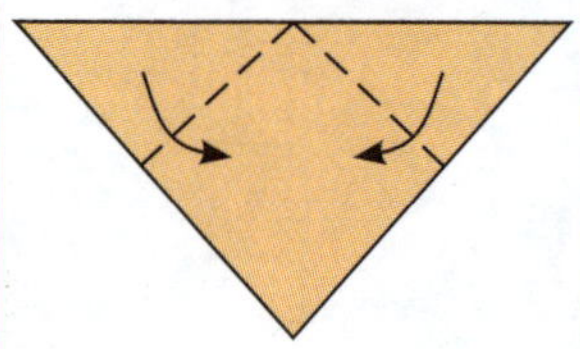

Step 4

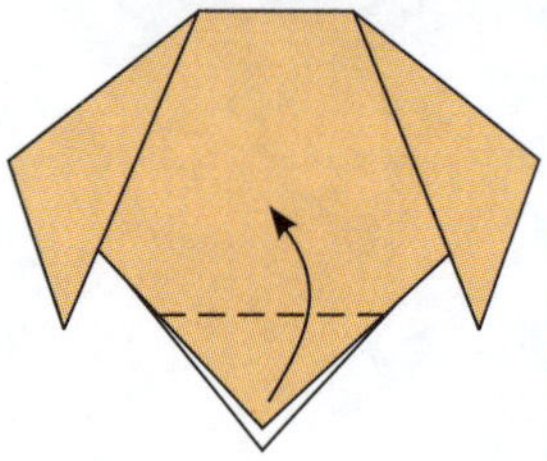

Step 5

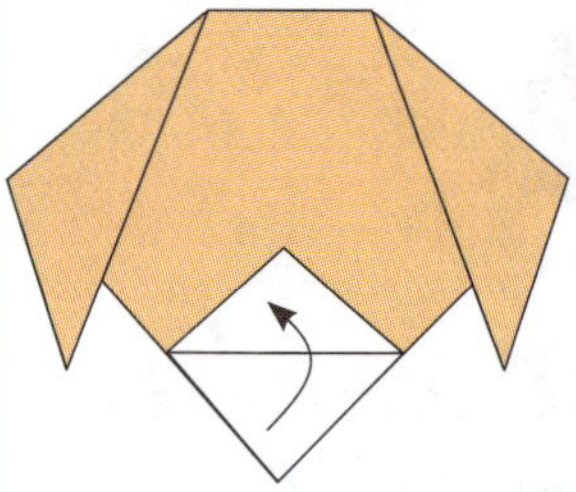

Step 6

Paste here

Procedure

Follow the steps to make the dog using origami paper. Use a black sketch pen to make the nose, whiskers and eyes of the dog.

Material Required

Origami paper, black sketch pen and glue

FLY BY BUTTERFLY

Paste buds of crayons on outer wings of the butterfly.

Procedure

Paste small or broken buds of crayons on the outer wings of the butterfly. Children can use stone/shiny stickers to decorate the inside wings.

Material Required

Small or broken buds of crayons, glitter, stone stickers and glue

DRIZZLING RAIN

Paste cotton on the cloud. Thumbprint 15 raindrops.

Procedure

Paste cotton within the outline of the cloud. Use a black sketch pen to outline the cloud. Dip the thumb in blue paint to print rain drops. Use black sketch pen to make eyes and smile for the cloud.

Material Required

Cotton, black sketch pen and blue poster colour

PEEKABOO

Find the hidden numbers and colour them blue. Colour and complete the picture.

WONDER WITH COLOURS

Colour the rainbow. Paste cotton to make clouds.

Procedure

Children should follow the correct colour sequence to make the rainbow. Paste cotton to make clouds.

Material Required

7 crayons—violet, indigo, blue, green, yellow, orange, red, cotton and glue

DRAW WITH NUMBERS

Draw and colour the woodpecker.

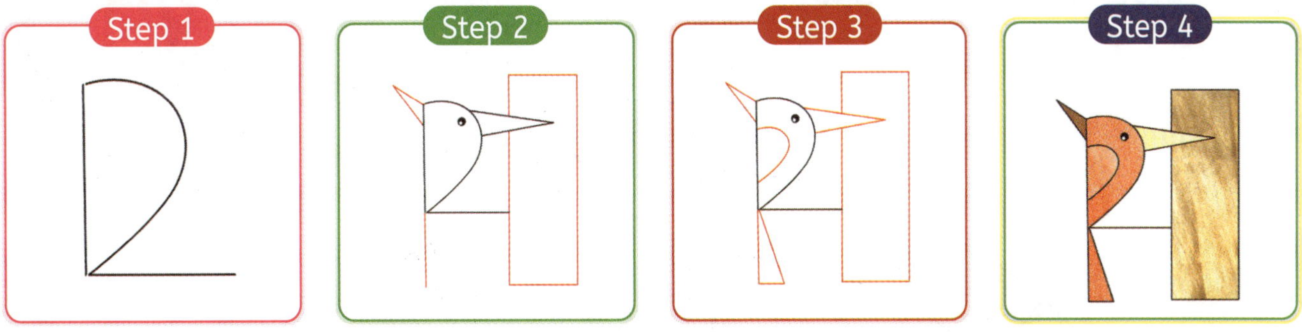

PIZZA TOPPING

Dip and print using ear buds to complete the pizza topping.

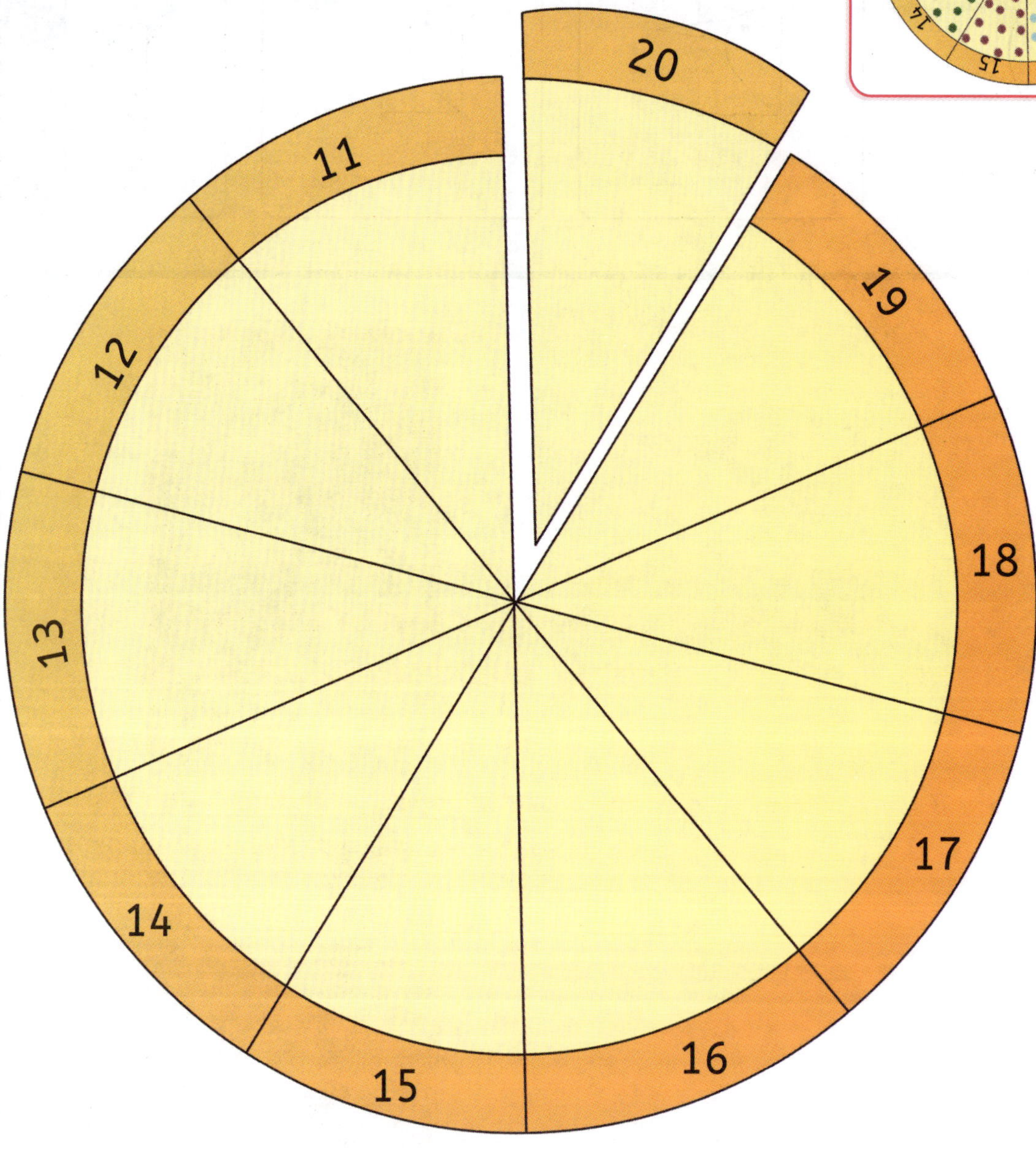

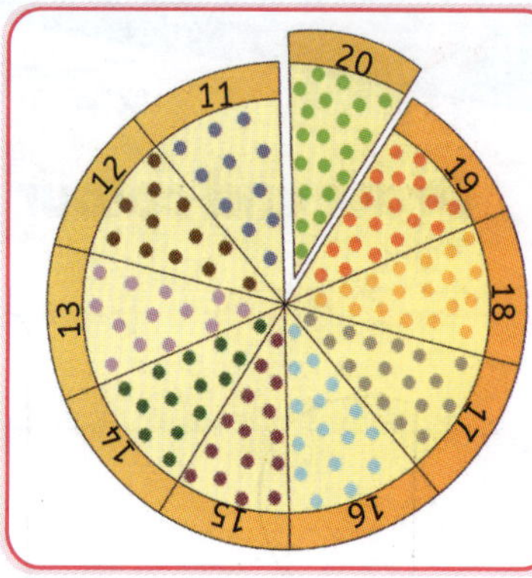

Procedure

Dip ear buds in a paint and print it on the sections of pizza. Make sure that each section of the pizza has same colour print.

Material Required

Ear buds and poster colours

LET'S DRAW!

Draw and colour anything you like.

HELLO LITTLE FISH

Use a coin to print scales on the fish.

Procedure

Take a coin and dip its edge in the paint. Now use the same edge of the coin to print the scales on the fish.

Material Required

A coin and poster colours

DRAW WITH NUMBERS

Draw and colour the squirrel.

BLOCK PRINTING

Take a piece of cotton cloth. Use a wooden printing block to print on the cloth.

Step 1

Step 2

Step 3

Paste here

Procedure

Dip the block in paint. Print on the cloth to make a pattern. Paste the cloth on the page.

Material Required

A piece of cotton cloth, acrylic paints, and a wooden printing block

OKRA PATTERNS

Use okra and different colours to make a pattern as you like.

Procedure

Dip the cut okra into any colour of your choice. Print to make a design.

Material Required

2-3 okras and poster colours

DRAW WITH NUMBERS

Draw and colour the whale.

READY FOR FUN

Use a long piece of yarn to make a colourful thread painting.

Step 1

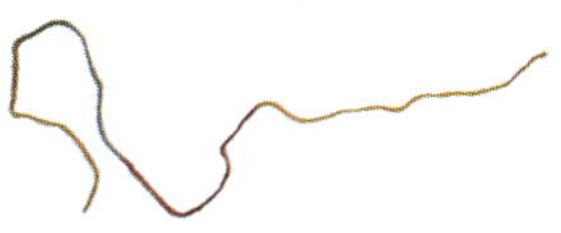

Step 2

Step 3

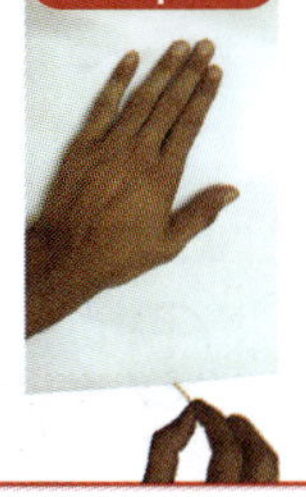

Step 4

Procedure

Take a long piece of string and dip its different portions in different colours such that each portion has a single colour on it. Press the thread along its length to remove excess paint from it. Fold the white paper in half. Open the paper and place the thread on one half of the paper with an end dangling outside the paper. Fold the paper again and pull the free end of the thread sharply but gently. You will see patterns on the page.

Material Required

A piece of string, square white paper and poster colours

LET'S DRAW

Draw and colour anything you like.

DRAW WITH LETTERS

Draw and colour the butterfly.

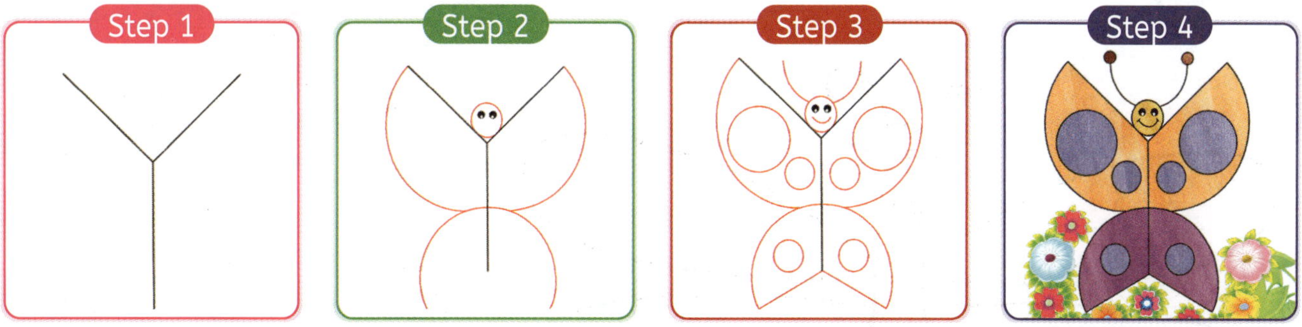

DANCING DRAGONFLIES

Make dragonflies with shiny stickers and sparkles.

Procedure

Children can colour the wings of the dragonflies and then use any shiny stickers and sparkles as they like to decorate the tails and wings of dragonflies. Use black sketch pen to make the eyes of dragonflies.

Material Required

Shiny stickers, glue and black sketch pen

DRAW WITH NUMBERS

Draw and colour the fish.

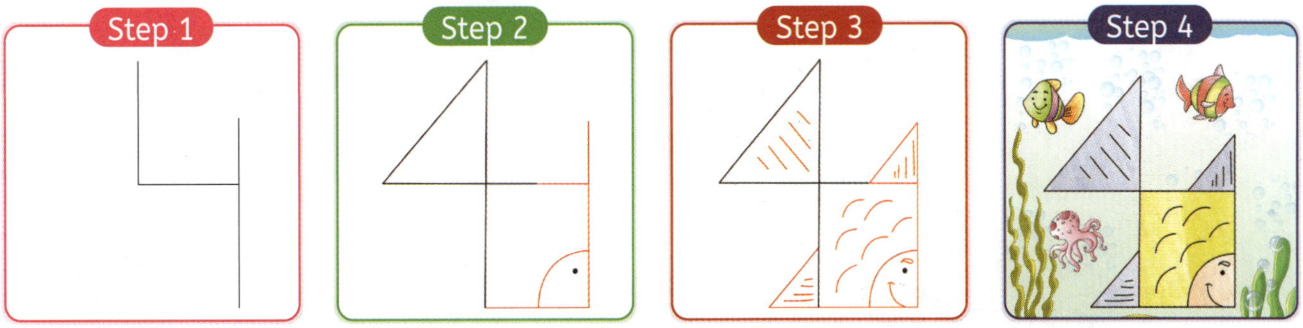

MY PRETTY FLOWERS

Paste yellow paper balls to complete the flowers.

Procedure

Take pieces of yellow crepe paper to make small balls. Pick one paper ball at a time and paste it on the hollow circles to complete the flowers.

Material Required

Yellow crepe paper and glue

COLOUR WITH CODES

Use the colour code and colour the picture.

LET'S DRAW!

Draw and colour anything you like.